CHALLENGE FOR A ROOKIE

CHALLENGE FOR A ROOKIE

A FIRSTHAND ACCOUNT OF SPRING TRAINING

BY DON BOLOGNESE

A THISTLE BOOK

Published by

GROSSET & DUNLAP, INC.
A National General Company
New York

To my father

ACKNOWLEDGMENTS:
I would like to express my thanks to my wife,
Elaine, and our two daughters, Marisa and
Anne, who helped in the preparation of this
book, and to the New York Yankee manage-
ment and players for their cooperation and
generosity.

Ever since I can remember, I dreamed of being a professional ball player. I liked both football and baseball, but my father and high school coach encouraged me to concentrate on baseball. That kind of support and interest from people I respected kept me going even when things got rough. Getting to the majors wasn't easy, but the effort has been worth it. Not only have many of my dreams come true, but I've learned a lot about life from the experience. And I guess the most valuable lesson I've learned is never to quit.

JOHN ELLIS

This is the story of a dream. It is a dream of power, skill, fame and fortune. It is the dream of being a major league ballplayer. When the calendar turns to February, that dream comes to life for the young ballplayers about to begin Spring Training.

Baseball had ended its winter hibernation. Rookie John Ellis was on his way to the Yankee training camp at Fort Lauderdale. He had been there last year but this year he felt he might make it all the way to Yankee Stadium—a place he had dreamed of all his life.

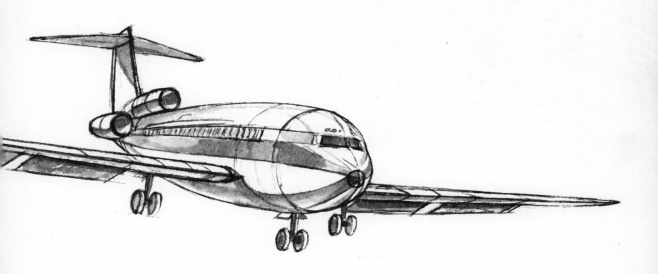

The jets zoomed into the airport carrying other hopeful young ballplayers, who only a few years earlier had been playing baseball in schoolyards. One of them, Rusty Torres, came from the streets and sandlots of Bedford-Stuyvesant in Brooklyn. And that is a long way from the beaches and palm trees of Florida. As the plane bounced on the runway Rusty, too, wondered how long it would be before he made it to the big leagues.

John Ellis walked onto the grass of Fort Lauderdale stadium on his way to the locker room. As he watched the palm trees swaying in the stiff breeze he thought of the fifty-six other players who were trying to make the team. Only twenty-five would be at Yankee Stadium on opening day. He knew that the baseball writers had called this group of ballplayers the best they had seen at Spring Training in seven years. There would be plenty of competition.

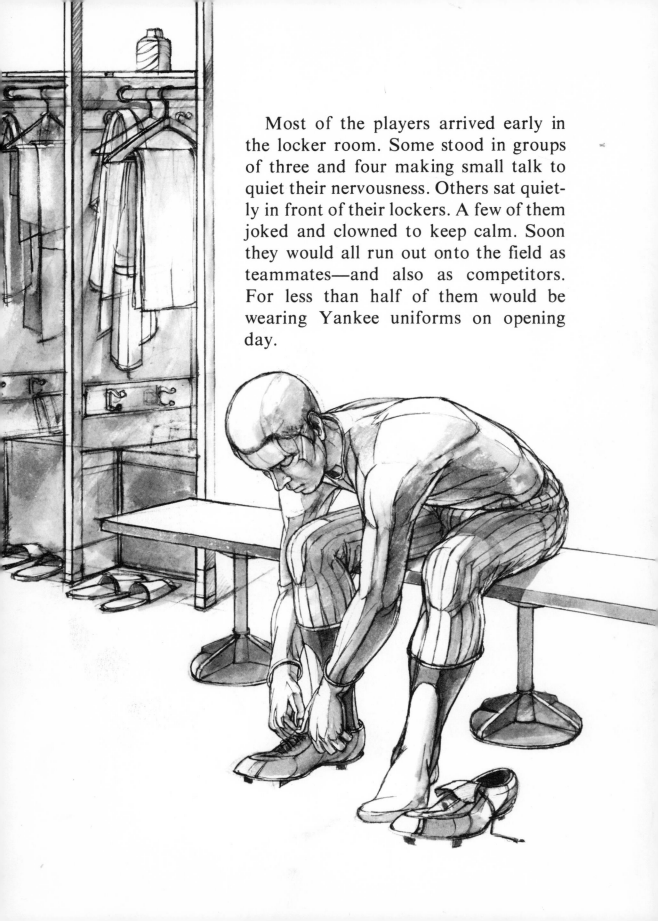

Most of the players arrived early in the locker room. Some stood in groups of three and four making small talk to quiet their nervousness. Others sat quietly in front of their lockers. A few of them joked and clowned to keep calm. Soon they would all run out onto the field as teammates—and also as competitors. For less than half of them would be wearing Yankee uniforms on opening day.

The sound of metal spikes on concrete vibrated in the dark tunnel that led from the locker room to the dugout. The players jogged quickly down the tunnel, up the two steps to the dugout, and out into the blinding sunlight of the field.

After a long winter, muscles were stiff, so each day of Spring Training began with a warmup run and exercises. Led by a veteran pitcher, the entire squad circled the field, stopping under the scoreboard. The leader began shouting "1-2-3-4-up-down-up-down."

Rusty felt his muscles stretch but he knew he must keep trim, keep his weight down; his agility and speed were valuable. "1-2-3-4"—the sweat was running now. The players all became impatient to play ball.

The squad broke up into two groups. The pitchers jogged off toward a second field to practice sliding. The pitchers laughed at each other's attempts, but they knew this was no joke. A bad slide could mean a broken wrist or leg, tough on any player but absolutely disastrous for a pitcher. An injury like that could mean the loss of a whole season—perhaps a career.

On the main field the other players were being put through basic fielding drills. John Ellis waited at first base for his turn at that position. He watched the catchers chasing bunts and foul pop-ups. He remembered when he had done the same thing for many hours.

"Big John" Ellis had come up to the minor leagues as an outfielder but the Yankees needed a catcher. So John was asked to try that position; it wasn't easy. He and his minor league coach worked for hours every day. Sometimes he was so discouraged he thought of giving up. But the Yankees' faith in him and his own hard work finally paid off. He did become a catcher. Now he was being asked to learn still another position—first base.

Once in high school, John had lost his position to another player. He had felt like quitting then too. But he remembered his father's words: "Lose like a man but never be a quitter." The crack of a bat, and John moved to his right, no longer thinking of anything but being a first baseman. A few more grounders, and another hopeful rookie took over his position. John went to the rack and picked a bat that felt good. He was up next.

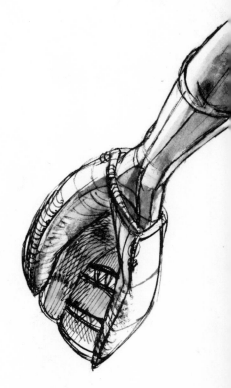

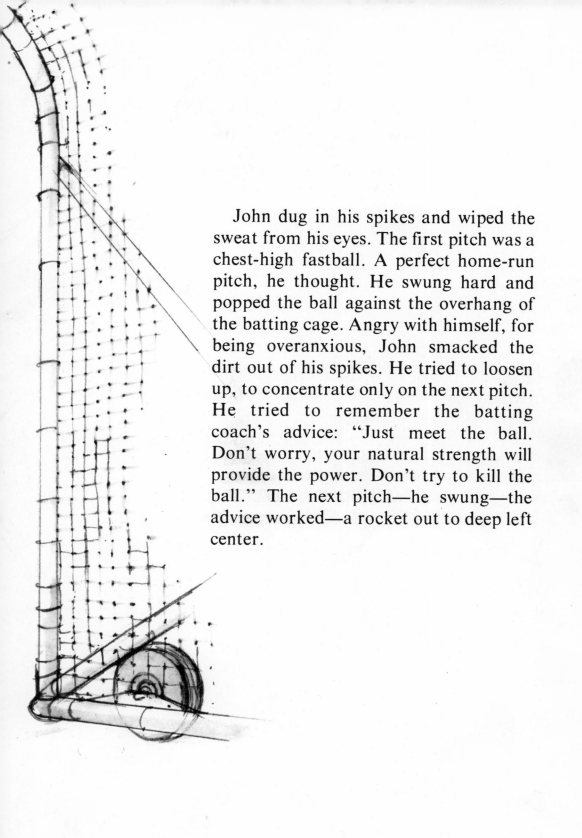

John dug in his spikes and wiped the sweat from his eyes. The first pitch was a chest-high fastball. A perfect home-run pitch, he thought. He swung hard and popped the ball against the overhang of the batting cage. Angry with himself, for being overanxious, John smacked the dirt out of his spikes. He tried to loosen up, to concentrate only on the next pitch. He tried to remember the batting coach's advice: "Just meet the ball. Don't worry, your natural strength will provide the power. Don't try to kill the ball." The next pitch—he swung—the advice worked—a rocket out to deep left center.

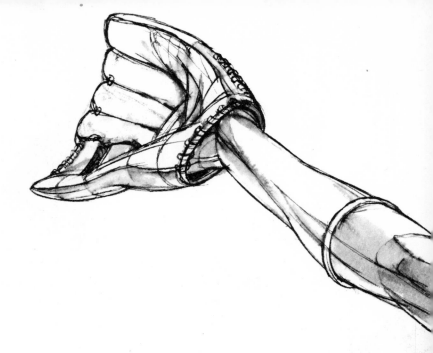

Rusty Torres raced to his right at the base of the centerfield fence and made a beautiful backhanded catch. A couple of other outfielders cheered him. But Rusty, like John and every other rookie in camp, was interested only in the opinion of one man—Ralph Houk.

From his seat behind the batting cage, Ralph Houk watched his team practice. And to make sure he missed nothing, he picked out three different players each day to study. What exactly was he looking for? Was it hustle? Talent? Was it baseball instinct—the ability to make the right move without thinking? It was all of these things. And experience! That's what turns a strong, talented rookie into a pro.

Manager Houk kept his eye on John Ellis. He knew this was John's third position since joining the Yankee organization. He understood the challenge facing John. There were eight players competing to play first base, most of them with more experience. But John would get plenty of chances to prove himself in the exhibition games.

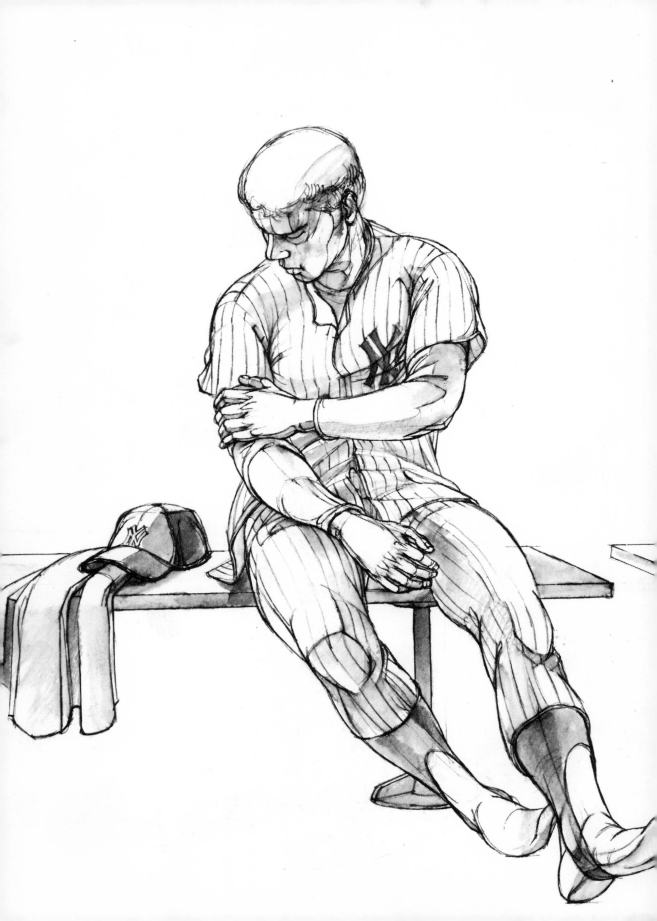

The first day of Spring Training was over. The players filed into the locker room. A light lunch was waiting for them; hot soup, raw carrots, celery stalks, hard-boiled eggs, juice and milk. A hot shower and a massage came next. The trainer and his staff would be very busy with sore muscles the first few days of Spring Training. But in two weeks when the games began, most of the squad would be in shape for the real competition.

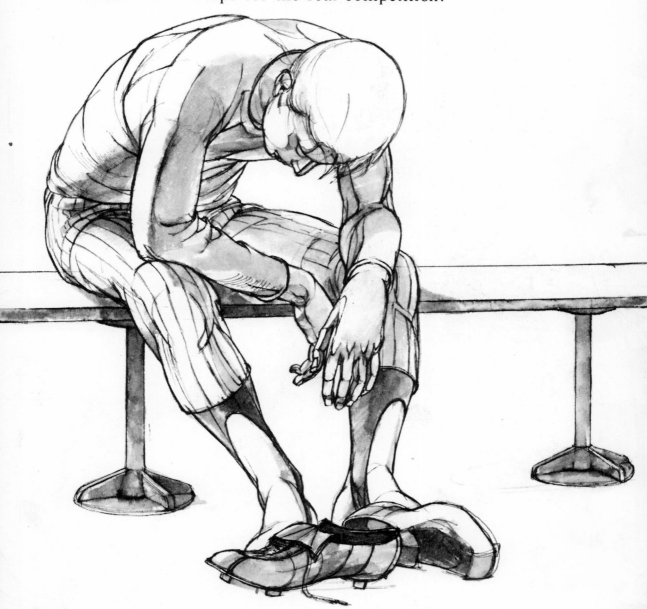

The drills were over. The first day of the spring exhibition games had finally arrived. The dining room had a different sound in the morning; the easy chatter between the ballplayers and the waitresses was gone. Rusty sat at a table, but he wasn't hungry. His thoughts were on the games—more than thirty of them. Would he get enough chances to play; to prove that he was ready for the major leagues? The other young players felt the same way. Most of them just stared at their pancakes. Soon the dining room was empty. The Yankee veterans and rookies were on their way to the ball park.

To the fans in the crowded grandstand it was only the first spring exhibition game. To the players it felt like the World Series. For this was their real chance to show what they could do. The umpire signaled for the teams to take the field. The game had begun.

It was a close game. In the ninth inning the Yankees were leading, 6-5. John, playing first base, felt the tension. He looked at the Yankee pitcher—another rookie. He had been pitching well, but now there was a runner on first base. The next batter was a rookie too, and according to the newspapers he was a slugger. John held the base against the runner. The pitcher threw . . . and by the sound of the bat John knew that the ball was high over Rusty Torres' head and into the palm trees outside the rightfield fence. The Rangers had won. John was disappointed. But tomorrow was another day and another chance.

The Yankees lost the next day and the day after. Then they began winning. The team started to take shape. Some of the extra pitchers and catchers were sent back to the minor league camps. Everyone else was playing hard whenever he got into a game—and trying just as hard to be patient when he had to sit on the bench.

About two weeks before the exhibition season ended, the squad was cut again. Rusty and several of the other players were asked to report to the manager's office. They knew what that meant. Houk tried to encourage them. Playing every day in the minors would make them better ballplayers than sitting on the Yankee bench for most of the season. He also reminded them that there was always the chance that they might be called up to the majors during the season. As each rookie went back to his locker, even that hope was no cure for his heavy disappointment.

John Ellis got the good word that day. He was fitted for his Yankee travel outfit. This meant he would be with the team at least until the final cut-off just before opening day. Two more weeks to prove he could be a Yankee.

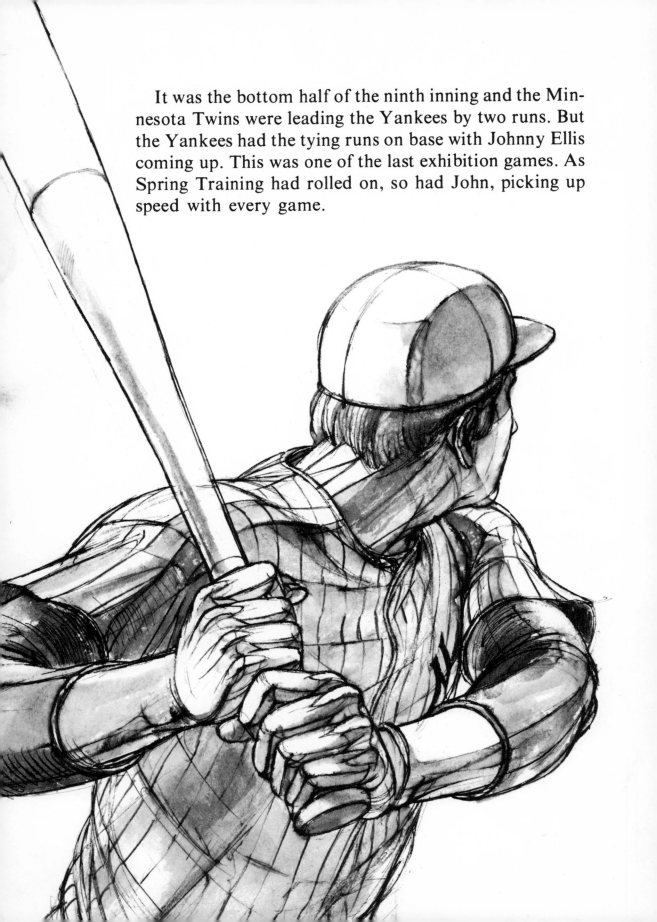

It was the bottom half of the ninth inning and the Minnesota Twins were leading the Yankees by two runs. But the Yankees had the tying runs on base with Johnny Ellis coming up. This was one of the last exhibition games. As Spring Training had rolled on, so had John, picking up speed with every game.

Now John stepped into the batter's box. The pitcher began his stretch. The first pitch—low and outside—ball one! John got set again—the pitch—he swung and fouled it back into the stands. The pitcher got a new ball. The next two pitches were balls. The count was 3-and-1 as John stepped back and looked toward the third-base coach. He got the signal. Ellis sensed the drama of the situation, but he wasn't nervous. Spring Training had given him the confidence he needed. He set himself again, dug in his spikes. The pitcher stretched; the runners led away; the pitcher's arm came up. It was a fastball. John timed it perfectly and sent it deep over the left center-field fence.

It was opening day at Yankee Stadium. John Ellis sat in the dugout with his teammates. The familiar faces filled him with a sense of friendship. He knew that all of them were rooting for him. He had felt the same when he received the James Dawson award as the best rookie of Spring Training. Mostly he wanted to live up to the hopes they had for him. He was anxious for the game to begin, and then it came—over the public address system as he had dreamed it a thousand times: "Batting fourth and playing first base, number 23, John Ellis . . ."

What Has Happened To John and Rusty Since 1970 Spring Training

John Ellis opened the 1970 season playing first base. For the remainder of the season he was platooned at that position playing mostly against left-handed pitchers. He batted .248 in 78 games. In 1971 he again shared the first base position batting .244 in 83 games. When the 1972 season opened, Jake Gibbs the Yankee back-up catcher retired so John became a catcher again. Although he played in fewer games (52), he improved at the plate batting .294 with 25 runs-batted-in.

Rusty Torres spent the 1970 season at the Manchester farm club. His career suffered from two serious injuries, torn knee ligaments and a broken wrist. However he made a strong comeback in 1971 with the Syracuse Chiefs, batting .290 and leading the International League in fielding with an average of .982. Rusty finally made it to the Yankees in 1972 where he played right field.

As the 1972 season ended, the Yankees needed a strong third baseman. They traded John and Rusty to the Cleveland Indians for the Indians' third baseman. This should give both of them an opportunity to develop their full potential.